Hounds *of* Wonder

A LIFE IN RESCUE DOGS

POEMS BY

B.D. Love

Hounds
of Wonder
A LIFE IN RESCUE DOGS

POEMS BY

B.D. Love

Hound of Wonder
Hound of Light
Hound of Royal
Beauty Bright

a marginally blasphemous
parody I always sang
to amuse Declan, the Wonder Hound,
who has proceeded Westward

This edition published by Highpoint Life.
For information, write to info@highpointlifebooks.com.

First Edition
ISBN: 978-0-9974157-4-2

Library of Congress Cataloging-in-Publication Data

Love, B.D.
Hounds of Wonder: A Life in Rescue Dogs

Illustrations by Walt Taylor
Cover and interior design by Amanda Kavanagh
Edited by Maura Kennedy

ISBN: 978-0-9974157-4-2 (paperback)
1. Poetry

Library of Congress Control Number: 2016958231

Contact B.D. Love:
c/o Bonificence Music
PO Box 1298
New York, NY 10276
Email: bdlove@bdlove.org
Web: bdlove.org

Manufactured in the United States of America
10 9 8 7 6 5 4 3 2 1

Dedication

To those that move — or dream of motion
— they who walk, swim, scurry, crawl, slink, leap, fly…
and dream… Dreams are motion. Motion is light.

Mostly, though, I dedicate this to my dogs,
with great love even in absentia.

"*Hounds of Wonder* is a strong, tender account of a life spent loving dogs. There is no doubt B.D. Love has mastered the art of the sonnet—each set of fourteen lines builds a unique little world around its canine subject. The gentle hints of Love's own life story add a human element and, overall, the collection is one that will move even those who are not particularly dog-lovers. To achieve what Love has in a form as restrictive as the sonnet is really remarkable."

—ELIZABETH GIBSON, *FOXGLOVE JOURNAL*, UK

"A compelling sincerity and kindness can be found in B.D. Love's *Hounds of Wonder: A Life in Rescue Dogs*. Love's sonnets are the work of a poet whose commitment to his craft is equal to his keen ability to chronicle the details of the lives of eleven very different dogs. These abandoned dogs live 'beside the freeway' or are 'trapped behind a chain link fence,' or caged in the 'Central Shelter' until they are rescued by the poet. This is a personal journey told by Love who feels the force of our human obligation to see how our culture has cast away so many dogs. Through the heartbeat meter of his sonnets, B.D. Love allows us to meet these beautiful, quirky, funny, shy and once cruelly treated dogs. In doing so, he reminds us that poetry is compassion and compassion is how we may rescue others."

—SUSAN COHEN, CO-EDITOR OF *COMING OF AGE AT THE END OF NATURE: A GENERATION FACES LIVING ON A CHANGED PLANET*

Other published works by B.D. Love/Lan Yan:

Punch Line (Short Fiction)
A Day in the Life of a Severed Head (Novel-in-Stories)
Song of the Ten Thousands (Novel)
DragonBlossom (Comedic Novel)
Water At The Women's Edge (Poetry)

Contents

Amuse-gueule

I've learned a lot from dogs, taught some, I guess,
Minor things like how to sit for a treat,
How to catch — a treat — and not to mess
Inside, well, just Declan, since after that

They've taught each other the dog door's sacred meaning.
I've never had much luck with heel or stay,
In truth, the treat does all the heavy training
When it comes to come. And then they walk away.

I've learned from them patience when I'm called to teach
My double-legged friends the basic drills
Of class, and when and not and what to scratch,
And whom, and that special bark reserved for fools —

But most of all, I've learned to lift a leg
To mark my turf, but also when to beg.

Tip I

Another dog, I think, predated you.
I never touched that one, swept from the house
And flipped to a farmer, someone I'd never know.
Dad in his day. I had to guess the toss.

What came to be in Chelsea, Michigan:
My father, bright, took my brother Mike
And me to a yard. These random pups were keen
Upon the basics. Licks. The stuff dogs make.

The stuff of dogs to come. I will recall
The way we walked through the creepy breeder's fence,
You were the last to come. The runt. I will
Imagine my finger pointing, me, the dunce.

The urge to search, to sniff, to run, to pant,
I owe to Tip. You did and still do grant.

Tip II

Relentless was you. I was a luckless kid,
Surveying woods and lakes, the water snakes
One side, the girls camp the other, which I did
Peruse, you in that rusty boat, upon the lake's

Pewter water at sundown. The muskrats roared
In Autumn, when the girls went back to where
They lived. I'd watch the sun set down and board
The boat and you'd really hammer the floor

Of that sad craft. We looked at cabins and dreamed.
Your Beagle black and tan, my tanning beige,
The rowboat's minor motor's roar — We gleamed
In birch and pine reflected light that would age

Into the winter, when snow would beard your snout.
My chin gets whiter, too, but I'm not out.

Tip III

You loved to eat the Crayons brother Mike
And I would use for pointless grade school projects —
Posters of saints, like Kennedy. Not Ike.
Because our school was strictly Cat'lick, subjects

Not in line with the Papal Wink: Taboo.
You had a fine disdain for authority.
(My lesson learned.) You went outside to poo
And winter times, the snow was deep, and we

We were just too chilled to clean the yard.
When spring arrived and snow began to wane,
The yard turned technicolor, every shard
Of Crayons — Purple Heart and Tangerine

Apricot, Amber, Sienna, Antique Brass.
You marked your neighborhood with more than piss.

Tip IV

The morning I awoke I knew it wrong,
I stuttered through the house. But you were gone.
The night before, you'd chewed a poster, a fang
Lashed out and caught my hand. This was a sign

To Mom, who never liked you anyway.
My sisters bent in sorrow, followed by Mom,
Returned at last. They said a neighbor — They
Lied: A neighbor poisoned you? The home

Was grim for weeks except, of course, for Mom.
My brother would not meet my eyes, my sisters
Withered. At midnight, dad would stumble, numb
From a dozen Martinis. The typical disasters

You had endured, and sought, in your way, to right.
The only voice you had was bark and bite.

Young
Declan

Declan I

You're slowing down these days. Your old back curves.
The muscles shrink beneath the sagging skin.
It's no surprise. Such is the way time carves
The marble block of life. We all begin

Solid and sharp, and end a pile of sand.
But I recall the eight-week-old that cried
And yelped beside the freeway fence. Abandoned.
I could have left you there, but I, afraid

To let another animal inside my life
And more afraid to feed you to the cars,
Bent down to snatch you up and make you safe.
You dug into and peed upon my arms.

I somehow drove you home, and you, once fed,
Surveyed your turf, then bit me so I bled.

Declan II

Lust is a must, as Ian Dury sang.
The only household male never to meet
The blades, you carried that weird red thing
Between your legs with pride. An acolyte

Of several Cardinal Vices (see above),
Luxuria remained your favorite.
You never met a curve you couldn't crave,
Which tipped the lady present into a fit.

Your shepherd markings gave you a saintly aura.
This helped you shake damnation, unlike the man
Who might at times glance at the local flora.
All dogs get into heaven. You loved that line.

Even creaking and senile, you tried to hump
Whatever. Sir, you went out like a champ.

Declan III

Anthropomorphize. I hate that term.
Ascribing human traits to something lower —
As if a dog would want to contract the germ
We call humanity. If I sound sour,

I am. I think about the time you charged
A dog double your size on the attack
Shot up the riverbank. Your heart enlarged
Your threat. That dog backed off. You saved your pack.

A canine bond isn't the loyalty
We humans think we own, but still it matters.
Show me a hero, I'll show you vanity
As many times as not. The right scar flatters.

You came back cut, you healed and, sure, you scarred.
For what that represents, I have no word.

Declan IV

I hold a photograph of you sitting in a box
Half-full of trim from the ancient pepper tree
Whose leaves would choke the eaves and drives and vex
The neighbor lady, who pleaded for the penalty

Of downing — this for a tree who shared her time.
She'd pass, pure white, beneath the "dirty" limbs.
"There's a fungus among us," my mom would chime
By way of warning. Indeed, there was. Death has her hymns.

But here you are, roots in the mulch, your face
Courting the camera's heart. The shutter clicks
And off you go to sniff all crones and grace
All trees with piss before a smaller box

Arrives to collect the last of the dust to fall.
Some old limbs creaked that night. I heard their call.

BooBoo I

The only sound you made was yelping when
Declan would round us up and drag us reeling
Down to the River. You, behind a chain
Link fence, alone all day, had found us failing.

We walked. You turned on your owner's living room,
Transforming drapes, carpet, sofa and seats —
All white — into a fecal Pollock, same
With the yard, which up you dug in sullen fits

Until you hit the water main, that geyser
Raining for hours on gasping passers by.
We passed, then turned, and waited. The neighbor, wiser
Perhaps, gave up. We took you home, where you lay

In the yard, content to gaze at a veil of blue,
A scrawny Shepherd angel silence drew.

BooBoo II

Nature is largely lost to us, except
For the potted plants we nurse — or, mostly don't —
Except for vermin, bugs and rats we've swept
Away like the nagging sins we won't repent.

Dogs, as the Monks of New Skete write, can offer
A glimpse into the animal soul that commends
The link between our world and theirs. I differ,
Not with the bond, with what and how it binds.

We braid the lands, shackle the winds and tides
And turn, ignoring the whole, the ways we task it.
I've met the heart that shapes, the hand that breeds
One dog to fill a cup and one a casket.

Why you were made, I doubt anyone cared.
But ours was pure as any love I've shared.

BooBoo III

I like my blasphemy straight up, as do
Most lapsing Catholics, so I'd drop a towel
Atop your head, Immaculate BooBoo.
Oh Virgin Hound! Bless us who've wandered AWOL!

You snug in the hole you dug, surrounded by sparrows
Subbing for angels — the other dogs, a cat
And a tortoise in for the saints — the photo borrows
From antique masters, though framed by a hypocrite.

At twelve, I took my Confirmation name —
Francis, Il Poverello, the animals' friend —
Poor choice for a boy who, faced with woods to tame,
Would bear the taint of all he b.b. gunned.

My saint earned holes in his feet and chest and palms,
But I earned you, to whom these words bear alms.

BooBoo IV

I'll remember you bounding along the riverbank,
Tramping patches of algae but never slipping
And rising green like the rest of us who stank
Of God knows what for days after the dipping.

I'll remember you leaping onto bed each night
To burrow beneath the sheets with us to follow
And mornings we awoke to find your snout
Beside my head or hers upon a pillow.

I'll remember your folding, your hips beyond repair,
The hopeless air of hope and resignation
That rose from your labored breathing — as if there were
A word that I could keep, an affirmation.

"We'll meet you soon," we hymned as you lay dying.
You closed your eyes, content that we were lying.

KIKO

KIKO I

In the ICU at LA USC
Our homeless friend from the River lay comatose,
Abandoned. The family Christianity
Did not apply to Richard's sorry mess.

The patient looked like a turnip, purple, white,
With tubes for stems. We stayed a while unseen.
Most of that time, I thought about the mutt
We passed at the entrance, asleep in the dirt, alone.

You were still there when we left. We paused. I mumbled
Something about a home. You rose from the dirt.
The guard just shrugged at our claim, and off we tumbled,
You at the lead, head up, unfazed, alert.

Richard would live, released to his rotten luck.
You'd never leave. Your heathen family stuck.

KIKO II

Maybe because you were a Scorpio
(Like me), you never ditched the mischief — that
Was the quality you'd never quite outgrow,
Unlike the collars and bedding. Your appetite

For chaos annoyed and amused. You loved the water,
Lured us — with friends in tow — into the River,
Where you'd paddle away, some oddball otter.
Later, you'd prance and shake. We'd gripe and shiver.

You mastered another water trick: The Zone.
An unsuspecting friend provided the game.
You'd fill your maw from your bowl like a cargo plane
And dump the load square in his crotch. His shame,

Your glee. And should he stand, you'd lunge and nip —
Toothsome revenge for the veterinary snip.

KIKO III

You dropped in the middle of any altercation
And let your bulk conclude the hostility,
Much as the sumo master's concentration
Disposes of foes with muscled gravity.

Good dog of peace, you'd never nip a finger
Although — I'm guessing here — that jaw could braid
A fist, if that was where you wrapped your anger —
If ever you got angry, which you never did.

My left hip went, so I, like you, have fought
The pain when bone, declining, chips and crumbles,
When pills rain down and fail and shots fall flat,
When rising bows and simple walking humbles.

You died on a mat at home. Your packmates hung
Around to know. We stood outside your ring.

KIKO IV

A favorite memory of you when small
And full of fire and roguery is when,
While artfully teething, you found the white steer skull
Lying beside the exercise machine.

This caused amusement, because a bone's a bone,
A pup's a pup, and your damage merely a glitch.
(I wish I had your finesse and could atone
For every felonious household nick or scratch.)

Who could resist your charm? Not neighbor kids
Who loved to poke your snout. Not kittens, who cuddled
Beside your belly while you groomed their heads.
With dogs, nature and nurture are pretty muddled.

Despite your routine Cubist home remodel,
We miss you cockeyed, Keke. Long may you idle.

Her name means brightness.

Phoebe I

When we arrived at the Central Shelter, you
Were last upon our list of dogs to adopt.
The online offerings were hardly few,
And we had sorted profiles and promptly flopped

Yours to the bottom of the stack. And there you were.
The only puppy not out on adoption day
At Corporation Pet. I could not bear
Your sickly self. And all the tech could say:

"Well, she can walk." You walked into the corner
And fell and pissed yourself. You smelled of the street.
Then you were ours. Your terror passed. The odor
Passed and you grew and grew, not the petite

Prediction, but one and a hundred twenty pounds
Of bark and heart. Now cancer makes the rounds.

Phoebe II

The death of a dog might seem a minor thing,
Some flesh, some bone, some blood — the catalog.
Often we weep about a broken wing
On a bird. I share that grief. But let's talk dog.

Phoebe is gone. It took just two injections,
One to the neck and one to the elbow joint.
She seemed at peace. I guess that some perfections
In life involve life's passing. A ragged tent

Unfolds, a carnival's arrived. The kids
Will spill from across the neighborhood and ride
Rides and think of nothing. A stray dog bids
For a cracker. Junk food. He's right, that dog, to bide

His time and improvise his nightly dish.
I think about my dog and make a wish.

Phoebe III

She had the face of a tough-guy pugilist:
Pug nose, the watery eyes, the underbite —
Some factions found her fearful. I guess the robust
Barking could cow the canine neophyte.

But she was all maternal. She ran this place.
She nudged the guinea pigs and scanned the cats
And moved with a clunky, darkly brindled grace
To run the other dogs back to their mats

And then she'd hop onto the bed and snore.
I think that snoring became her way to tame
The room of mammals. We couldn't sleep, the roar
Pervasive, but that was Phoebe. You'll learn her name

Means brightness, and though in the end, the lingering light
Came mainly through those eyes, it still rang right.

Phoebe IV

The roses endure within their forlorn vase,
A blur of yellow, white and pink atop
The casual green. It may be flowers erase
Some loss: A grandma gone. The mortal glop

Turned chalk by some mortician's alchemy.
Then flowers. Phoebe, you meteored to ash.
You're in a box, but I claim memory.
Your puppy whimper, the overwhelming wash

Of smoke from where you came. We cleaned up good.
You followed me along the river, ears
Set wide for sounds of gunshot, the banging 'hood.
That street will calculate my mundane fears.

The bark, our bark – we howl at the edge of days.
From roses, a swallowtail ascends her breeze.

Silvi

Silvi I

You came from the street, hid out in a corner park
And didn't much take to light domestication,
Preferring the "outdoor life" to "traditional work."
My kind of dog. Welcome to Chaos Nation.

You looked something a mini-Husky bore
With a Shepherd. You didn't run. You hopped.
And what about that ear? A competitor
Bit off a thumb-sized chunk. He must have cropped

The part that caught the word behave, as you
Appeared to recognize most language — treat,
For instance: Dinner. Vet. Good girl! But do
When I said don't, and no meant now. Too late

To change you, once you hip-hopped through the door.
We'd lay the line: Enough. Translation: More.

Silvi II

You and cats. Damnit — a stereotype
In my damned house? Poo wouldn't tolerate
Canine shenanigans — nope, not a nip.
But she was gone and buried before you hit

The neighborhood's unwitting stage. The fur
Indeed, did fly whenever you'd discover
A tabby cowering beneath a bush in fear.
Your tiny pointed snout became a lever

To pry up, flip and toss the shrieking prey
Into a sort of somersault and when
It finally dropped, you, with a juggler's eye,
Snapped up its neck — and away it flew again.

Back home, you'd find your special spot and lie,
Paws crossed in wide-eyed, hopeless symmetry.

Silvi III

It's always the wrong time and it's always wrong.
Factual, yes, but wrong. That time to die.
You had a couple days before your clock would spring.
Calls made and calls returned. It's nature's way.

The vet intoned. You'll want to take her home.
You limped to your special spot, and you'd remain,
Breathing in fits, until the moment came.
You stood at the bedroom door, alive with pain,

But wearing the face you'd save for the evening wind.
You know, your packmates knew all things as well.
I bent to stroke your head. You licked my hand.
The stainless table, the antiseptic smell,

The needles poised at attention — they'd wait their turn.
I sat and stayed, commands you'd never learn.

Silvi IV

Your name came from the Latin word for woods,
A root I hadn't recalled. I simply listened.
Dogs tell us stuff, sure as they show their moods.
The cynic scoffs, but it's true. First call, you hastened,

A trick you'd never repeat, obedience.
You raced the pack up the dusty trails,
Devouring pine and eucalyptus scents,
Meeting the long and lonely coyote calls —

Teasing the brush to stir a rattler's warning.
One never hit. You flicked off death, unmoved.
Death came. For months, your spirit lingered, morning
And dusk. A flimsy silvan shadow shaved

The edge of a glance. I recognized that dust:
The dog who'd never heed the go in ghost.

BRIAN

Brian I

The cone you're forced to wear to stop your licking
The self-inflicted wound on your left rear knuckle
Made me consider whether the vets were cracking
Up as they fit that thing. I'm tempted to heckle.

It looks like a lateral, inverted dunce's cap.
Does this signal a genius — or half of one?
I'm sure you're not much flattered by either rap.
From the first, you kept some dignity, your zone.

As the others sniffed and circled, prodded and tried
Your patience, they no doubt wondered, who is this clown?
Well, Declan, BooBoo, KIKO and Silvi did
Their costume time; Your younger packmates — when,

Not if. Don't look so glum. You're not alone.
Sooner or later, everyone gets the cone.

Brian II

A dog is a thing of joy — the platitude
True in the main. A dog can culture penance
As well. Your oddly rounded frame and head
Recall a dog for whom I read the sentence.

Stupid with youth, a kind of love, and gin
I let poor Bosco out, and he got hit.
That's Dallas — Home of the pickup limousine,
City of shit and lead for brains and feet.

You vex me, Brian — snap when I offer snacks,
Develop a way to turn your protective cone
Into a corrective device, scoring the backs
Of my legs. A weak reminder, pain for pain.

Your lash is clean. Mine leaves a ragged cut.
For what it's worth, for us, I keep doors shut.

Brian III

Love at first lick. I knew myself in you.
She guessed that I'd prefer you be returned —
No refund, sorry — to the dude without a clue
Who found you, lost — or keep you, mileage earned.

I'll always keep my strays and never expect
Reward somewhere along the line. Don't laugh.
That's me, the clueless husband dude who cracked
The code when her hiking partner suitor oaf,

Invited for lunch time and again, would smack
Your sides with sweaty, drooling, witless force.
She just stood there as you stood in and took
The idiot whacking meant for me, of course.

He phoned one final time. She nursed his wailing.
We beaten went away, dog sense prevailing.

Brian III.I

I was chewing smog with a local politician,
Something about a crime, the potholes, trash,
And you slipped out the door, you canine magician.
At least you didn't halve the wife, or lash

A plume of dove from a burst of fire. You scooted.
I shrugged back in the house and you weren't there
And then I panicked and then the phone was dotted
With a stranger's number, and there your ass was where?

Somebody's street. It's not that you're getting senile
(Redundant, since nothing always winds up nothing).
Just that you wanted to strut along awhile,
Sniff old sad butts, nuzzle a cute chick's clothing.

The finder offered a leash. I grabbed your scruff.
You snorted once. That's politics enough.

Brian IV

The weak holds together the powerful.
I asked I Ching to comment on you. He did:
The judgment fits, of course. Not sorrowful
With age, you curb evil, further the good.

You look more Buddha than Confucius — I see
The Golden You meditating beneath
The computer station, the current Bodhi tree,
And wish to rub your belly. The raging youth

Ripens with time into a sad blancmange,
A pudding of flavorless regret or, say
A killer king in corporate camouflage.
The sage is a dog who follows the middle way.

Francis, our saint, wore rags and you, mere hide.
Truth is accessible, but dignified.

Alex

Alex (Alejandra) I

You move like a vowel, the softer kind we drawl
To hold a thought until it finds its way.
In the shelter photograph, your eyes were full
Of languishing hope — could it be me? — That day

Was underlined in red, like something hot.
It was and wasn't. You came home to me,
To us. It took some weeks, but you forgot
The consonant of cold captivity.

The desperate, empty cage again will swell.
A dog will signal the longing night and I
Will add an angry clang damning to hell
The misnamed human being who sired your cry.

Alex, you sleep in contented silence true
As sounds can never be. That face. Oh you.

Alex (Alejandra) II

Seduce, secure, sedate — sounds military,
A plan some sweatless generals might devise
To neutralize a neutral adversary,
A slogan the spinning ilk can advertise.

It's really just a common marriage arc,
Observed clear-eyed by Welles in Citizen Kane:
The gaps between the dinner silver mark
The space between the couple. Love, laid plain.

We are not even married, dog. What's up
With slinking off to a different couch whenever
I plunk my sad ass down and pat your hip,
Looking for affirmation, just a sliver?

You've learned a trick, and it's got legs. Two legs —
You've doubled down. At least the tail still wags.

Alex (Alejandra) III

I'm odd man out in weekly therapy.
Distant and disinclined to add my own
To the general reservoir of misery,
I'm glad when the self-inflicted bonding's done.

You make more sense. You don't sweat the denial
Or relapse watching the talking dead reflect
On future fossils hooked on fossil fuel.
You just do stuff. Not that you don't suspect

What's on the hoof. But you've a hand to lick,
A bowl to empty. Love and food, that's it,
Mainly. Add a walk, toss in a stick
To chase — you've got a life. You learned to sit,

Pure gold to delight the most despairing master
Adapting that trick amid this life's disaster.

Alex (Alejandra) IV

The way that Mohawk cowlick roils the fur
Behind your ears and down the back of your neck
Belies the terminal elegance you bear,
The face and form that wreck the usual ships:

The woman who points you out and gasps — how cute! —
While the shrieking child in tow makes a caboose
Behind her skirt — or the hapless, cross-fired brute
Who takes his ganders but never get a goose —

He'll get his just deserts — read: none — that night,
Having diverted his glance toward the leash's
Mother node as his wife reared back to bite.
Good luck, asshole. Enjoy the eyelash lashes.

Such is the mayhem beauty incarnates —
Domestic here, but chaos radiates.

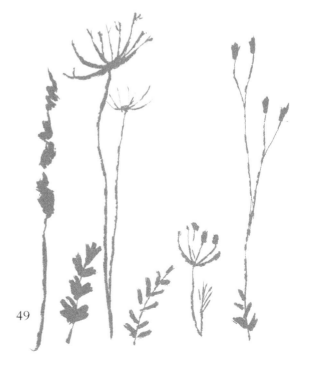

49

Krista

Krista I

Murder by shelter, dodge as we do, is murder.
There's always someone seated in another room
To scratch his steely name a little harder
Each time above a line. This is how shame

Dissolves into an antiseptic haze.
The number twenty thousand dead goes down
Smoothly enough. Some forty thousand eyes
— A parade of zeros — This in LA alone.

The killing's less like Vietnam than Iraq.
No scalding children etched into the lens,
Just sandy sketches fading to shadow black.
You beat both fates. You dodged the ruddy pens

And, hardly a blur, you daily coalesce —
One hyper, awkward, beautiful golden mess.

Krista II

My mother said, "You buy somebody's car,
You buy somebody's trouble." You are a dog,
Of course, and came for basic tender, the fur
And fret included. Trouble? You bring it big.

What you can't steal and bury you'll gladly tear.
My darling fluffy broken gyroscope,
The only dog I know on Prozac, where
Were you? In some fool's yard, tied by a rope

To a pole, circling until the noose closed tight
And your breathing became a perpetual desperate pant?
The other dogs have learned to tolerate
You, not to love. I do. We share a want.

You follow me around. I sneak you treats,
Something to fill an emptiness that eats.

Krista III

I am the sitting dork who came between
The teeth of you and Phoebe. Jealousy
Had reared the lovely head without a brain,
Instinct commandeering intimacy.

One golden streak from the left, one black and tan
From the right. Then damage. The ER doctor joked
My days as a hand model were over. Damn.
Cleaned up, the ripping healed. No blame invoked,

No wrath incurred. But the ivory scar tattoo
Adorning my shoulder never fades. I fault
The gaping hatch, the vacant driver. The crew
From the market mopped as the culprit tried to bolt,

Accusing innocent me to spare her honor.
Free the Doberman. Quarantine the owner.

Krista IV

One half of you goes here, the other there —
You bump your counterparts until they're pissed
And snap at the chaos cloaked in yellow fur.
You haven't got a malicious bone. It's just

Your bones seem not connected all that great.
And so you panic and so the mess gets worse.
Your eyes tear up. You want to do what's right
And every step goes wrong — but when, like a horse,

You bolt and run, your wayward lines converge
Into a streak and then a point of grace.
You gallop, bound — an elemental charge
Informing your limbs and ghostly lovely face.

Some bodies take to earth. You take to air.
Your landing's what it is. And I don't care.

Krista IV.I

I never had to kill a dog for lack
— Now this is very hard — Of being a dog.
Krista could not contain an urge to attack
Anything. She'd never listen nor log

A command. It wasn't just the other hounds
She'd get into skirmishes with. She went for death.
And without a notion. Time to kill. The rounds
Of ripped up ears, clipped coats. The epitaph:

Krista was made, and she couldn't be un-made.
She met me every morning, delirious
That I'd awakened again. And she'd parade
Out back like a show horse. Then came the typical mess,

Two gals. One knows to sit. One strikes. Wrong trick.
Collateral tossed from a sterile needle's prick.

Hansel

Hansel I

You came here chopped. Some fool had docked your ears
And tail, then tossed you from his car into
The street, still wearing his butcher gloves. His tires
Burned as he sped away, and tiny you

Wandered the asphalt until a neighbor cared.
And then I cared. And you were mine. And now
You race about the house, a puppy herd —
Blitzing the other dogs. Dark bullet, go.

It hardly matters you're an omnivore
Of furniture. The dollars tumble, but
You love your mayhem, love to shake and tear
Apart your bed and toys. I'll take the bait

Each time you crouch, your barracuda stare
Fixing my toe and the bone you dropped. You dare.

Hansel II

It's yeah, all right, it's you. It works that way.
The magnetic inevitability of love
Is overrated. You are my dog, dog. You stay.
And then you sit and fetch and forever behave.

Not so, so much. We're more about some time.
It nips the heels of the brave and aggrieves the slacker.
The furniture you gnawed? Some good god damn
When you turned the antique oak to brand-new wicker.

After a trauma severe as a finger wagged
And a you! you bad, bad boy, you got the picture
Quicker than the young tree rat you snagged
And dropped upon the kitchen floor. A stricter

Fool than I would've struck with his mad dog eyes.
Tail to the pail. Or not. As love, thus wise.

Hansel III

You and I stand in agreement: cats
Are weird. They're smart and all, got game (and how! —
They dribble hapless prey in casual fits),
Appear to love, although you never know —

Their little brains aren't wired like yours and mine.
We tend toward sloppy hugs, like the Democrat.
They're more the standard model Republican.
They'll purr, but only until their needs are met.

You'll never change a cat, no matter how
Airtight your logic, how dead-on are your facts.
This bone's my bone, you bark. They'll just meow
Some platitudes, look bored, and show their backs.

But Boots at her plate beside you at your bowl
Insinuates détente is possible.

Hansel IV

You are, you'll always be a momma's boy.
I tried that once. It didn't resolve so great.
But raise a leg to the life ahead, I say —
Go for it all, Hanse, by caveat —

Don't let the bastards cut your trajectory —
A fitting image since you've gotten fat
And look like a bomb or a bullet, little guy.
The world's your target. First, though some weight.

I've counted out a wealth of decades now
In dog years, judging my traits by theirs, the damned
The blessed, in Declan, BooBoo, Silvi, 'KO,
Brian, Alex, Krista and you. This hand,

Living, I hold it to you, my arc and span.
See here. The pup is measure of the man.

Gretta

Gretta I

The blur you were, a snapshot afterthought
Hastily slapped on a mingling site: A stray,
Found wandering cold and lonely late one night...
Betting a void on an amber smudge, our way,

We sent a sleek reply and you, delivered,
Scored home. Your predecessor's spirit sighed
In the backyard dirt and leaves she'd always favored.
A fox replacing a wolf. No choice. She's dead,

Krista, and though you lie against the wall,
Her spot, paws up, like hers, you are not her.
You shouldn't be. It's just, the ease of it all,
The sleek delete, the quick refresh, the fur

On all passes, not ashes to ashes, dust
To dust, but bits to bits, and ghost to ghost.

Gretta II

I get it now. You're not a dog to miss
A beat. I'm sad about the squirrel you
Apparently just put to rest. The piss
And vinegar of some old breeding, true

To your genes. We're pretty all like that.
I fought the law and the law won. That song
Keeps filtering in, except you're winning. The heat
Of daily joy, the instinct, killer and wrong

Sometimes, the you of you. I look at me,
Not much in the general matrix. I have some words
That will not resonate as brilliantly
As when you bark at that stray raccoon that hoards

The outside food for cats. This wilderness
Within a city where I remain amiss.

Gretta III

Your sandy colored fur reminds me much
Of the beach where you were rescued: covered with mud,
Afraid, and then, in days, you trotted, rich
With promise. A new pet makes an old heart thud.

That's pretty much the way it works with change.
The heart just clunks, and then restarts again.
Your leaps, your twists, the way you rearrange
The pillows, sheets, the floor, the chairs…a sane

Person, this not being me, in likelihood
Would fear the the troubles that might brew. You knew
I'm brave enough, and now you rule the bed.
I love and therefore am. The philosophers brew.

Tough from the start and tougher later, friend.
That sidewise canine grin: Don't let it end.

Gretta IV

You lie upon the bed, back down, legs spread
Inviting the midsummer breeze to cool you down,
I'd guess. I am no dog. Well, truth be said,
I am, but a gal you've met has tamed this clown

Of a canine. You perk when you hear her name. I do
As well, reciting it almost endlessly.
I think I've trained myself. How that went through,
I think it's love. But she is she and we

Have met and now one disciplinary tap
Upon my neck, behind my ear, defines
A solar spinal tingle. Gretta, you nap
And should. I'm warm. My sleeplessness inclines.

Believe in all impossibilities,
My hound. I try. Look to my windswept eyes.

Desservir

Beware the man who is not moved by dogs.
Beware the woman, too. Sometimes she's worse.
They sputter through life, these human analogs,
Denizens of a parallel universe,

Denying more than half a million years
Of happy symbiosis never occurred.
These are the folks who believe the dinosaurs
And Mankind walked as friends. Thus sayeth the Lord.

(Likely while drunk, from what we know of him.)
From similarly bone-schooled minds, this staple:
Dogs being wolves will work for blood. Look, Jim:
Wolves do not eat people. People eat people.

I choose the pack and not the swarm of flies.
Maybe I see the world through canine eyes.

70

Acknowledgements

Thanks to *Nimrod* for first publication of "Declan IV." We're graced here with the luminous illustrations by Walt Taylor, who captured the spark of each hound's soul. Maura Kennedy blessed the volume with her editorial insights and considerations, even as the hounds came to wonder. J Bruce Jones and Michael Roney both stepped in to generously offer advice and mentorship just as we lost similar guidance from our dear friend and mentor, Jack Lamplough. Amanda Kavanagh graciously and gracefully provided the cover and interior design. Thanks as always to Jay Rogoff, for his many years of support, suggestions and, in many cases, sheer clairvoyance.

In memory of Jack Lamplough, 1957—2016.

About the Author:

B.D. Love is a poet and novelist with over a hundred poems published in various literary magazines, as well as four books of poetry and four novels to his name. He has been nominated for many literary awards, including most recently for the Pushcart Prize: Best of the Small Presses in 2013 for poetry, and for the National Book Critics Circle Award 2012 for his novel *A Day in the Life of a Severed Head*. B.D. has taught English Composition and Creative Writing at California State University of Los Angeles for thirty years, mentoring and serving as Faculty Advisor to several groups including the Creative Writing Club, and as designer and editor of the *Creative Writing Club Journal*. In addition, B.D. Love has been involved in many community service organizations and events, specifically benefiting the Pasadena Humane Society and the Friends of the Los Angeles River.

About the Illustrator:

Walt Taylor is a freelance artist/designer in Norfolk, Virginia. He loves drawing all kinds of subjects, especially animals for friends.

.

Lightning Source UK Ltd.
Milton Keynes UK
UKOW07f0740190417
299363UK00013B/72/P